THE MEANINGS OF MODERN ART

by JOHN RUSSELL

Art Critic, *The New York Times*

VOLUME 9

A LOST LEADERSHIP

THE MUSEUM OF MODERN ART, NEW YORK

I. Pablo Picasso
Three Musicians, 1921
The Museum of Modern Art, New York

Series ISBN 0-87070-477-X Volume 9 ISBN 0-87070-486-9 Designed by Earl Tidwell
Cover: plate VI. Pierre Bonnard, *Nude in Bathroom*, 1932. The Museum of Modern Art, New York

Something was lost to Europe in the first half of this century that can never be put back again.

This is not a matter of physical destruction—though nothing can restore the look of the European countryside before industrialization, or of Dresden and Warsaw, Rotterdam and the City of London, before World War II. It has nothing to do with economics: most people in most parts of Europe live better than ever before. It has nothing to do with world domination: not many young people mourn the days when Great Britain ruled India, when much of Africa was dominated by Germany and Italy. and when France and Holland had fiefs in Southeast Asia. If western Europe is moving toward federation, that too is all to the good; we can only rejoice if a war between France and Germany now seems hardly more likely than a war between New Hampshire and Vermont. A great many exceptional individuals withdrew from Europe after 1930—among them Einstein, Mondrian, Schoenberg, Mies van der Rohe, Thomas Mann, Stravinsky—but the loss which I have in mind is not of them. It is of a more general and a more fundamental sort.

What was lost to Europe between 1900 and 1950, and above all between 1939 and 1945, was the sense of predestined leadership which had been taken for granted since the days of Plato and Virgil, Charlemagne and the builders of Chartres Cathedral. It was to everyone's advantage—or so it had seemed to those who had the power—that the world should be run by Europeans. European ethics, European systems of law, European science, European medicine, European organization and the European capacity for disinterested enquiry were self-evidently superior to all others; when a European of the class of 1880 read that God had created Man in His own image he put down the book and said, "He was thinking of ME—and he did a pretty good job."

In political and social terms this total assurance was somewhat battered by the end of the 19th century. But in literature, music and the arts the heroic age of modernism—1905 to 1914, let us say—did much to confirm it. A minority of far-seeing natures had sensed that there might have to be, at the very least, some radical adjustments: what is put before us in Thomas Mann's *Death in Venice* (1912) is not the death of a middle-aged man of letters but the death of a certain idea of Europe. (Europe might not, that is to say, have all the answers. Beauty could destroy, as well as uplift, and plague could break out where nothing had been foreseen but exalted pleasure.) Nor could an intelligent reader of Joseph Conrad's *Heart of Darkness* (1902) fail to sense that the European domination of distant and alien peoples was entering upon its terminal phase. But the general tenor of life during the heroic age of modernism was affirmative: looking at Picasso's

Les Demoiselles d'Avignon (1907; Volume 4), listening to Stravinsky's *The Rite of Spring* (1913), admiring the lucid disentanglements of human oddity in Sigmund Freud's *Totem and Taboo* (1913), feeling our way into the first volume (1913) of Marcel Proust's *Remembrance of Things Past*, we recognize in every case a determination to master the new dimensions of human nature and, by mastering them, to keep Europe on top.

Such was the density of European achievement before 1914, such the sense of shared energy, and such the imperiousness of the historical logic which prompted a breakthrough in one domain after another, that in comparison the achievement of the 1920s and '30s is bound to seem dispersed, occasional and unsystematic. A four years' war is destructive of moral energy; D. H. Lawrence put that point in *Aaron's Rod* (1922) when he said that after World War I Europe was like a soldier in shock, outwardly unhurt but in reality "wounded somewhere deeper than the brain." Before long what the French thinker Julien Benda in 1927 called *La Trahison des clercs*—the betrayal of society by those best fitted to guide it—had come to characterize every department of European life; politically, morally, economically, Europe was decaying, hour by hour. It should not surprise us that at such a time the masters of the modern movement decided, one after another, to take stock of the European tradition and to see how much of it was worth preserving and restating and how much might as well be thrown away.

There was in all this an element of fastidious differentiation. If the proceedings had sometimes a touch of Savonarola—all fire, all ice, all righteous condemnation—there was much more of Montaigne, and of Montaigne's delight in turning over the facts one by one, at leisure and without prejudice. To painters like Bonnard and Braque, and to a sculptor like Brancusi, today's craving for instantaneous approval would have seemed both childish and self-defeating; one of the things that they had inherited from the centuries of European hegemony was the right to a privileged silence.

The Rumanian-born sculptor Constantin Brancusi is, in fact, a very good example of this. Brancusi was born in 1876 in the humblest of circumstances in a farming village in the foothills of the Transylvanian mountains. From the outset of his career he was clearly very gifted; but when he decided to go to Paris in his middle twenties he was so poor that he had to walk almost all the way. He was quickly recognized—by Apollinaire, by Matisse, by Léger, by Marcel Duchamp—as someone quite out of the ordinary; but although Paris remained his base till his death in 1957 he never had a one-man exhibition there. His first one-man show was in New York in 1914. The photographer Edward Steichen

1. Constantin Brancusi
The Kiss, c. 1912
Philadelphia Museum
of Art

In portraying the embraces of his well-matched but undeniably paunchy pair of lovers (fig. 1), Brancusi presented an ever more stylized variant of the idea that in the act of love man and woman become one flesh. In this version, the confrontation is literally "eyeball to eyeball." The woman's breasts, stomach and knee-length hair are delicately suggested, but the emphasis is on the completeness of the union—whence the locked lips, the identical blocklike form of the heads, and the paired and flattened arms which encircle the central mass as straps encircle an old-fashioned suitcase.

2. Constantin
   Brancusi
   *Magic Bird
   (Pasarea
   Maiastra),*
   version 1, 1910
The Museum
   of Modern Art,
   New York

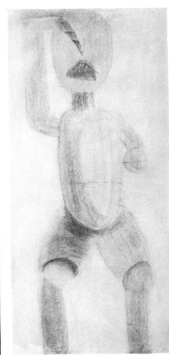

3. Constantin Brancusi
The First Step, 1913?
The Museum of Modern Art,
   New York

4. Constantin Brancusi
*Figure (Little French
   Girl),* 1914–18?
The Solomon R. Gug-
   genheim Museum,
   New York

The *Maiastra* (fig. 2), familiar to all Rumanians through their native folklore, was a golden-feathered bird with magical properties. It could cure the sick and the blind. It could out-sing the nightingale. It could even bring back the dead to life. In this, it was the descendant of the solar birds which figure in many ancient cultures. Brancusi may well have been reminded of it, as the art historian Athena T. Spear has suggested, both by the publication of a long poem on the subject in Bucharest in 1909 and by the first performances in Paris in 1910 of Stravinsky's ballet *The Firebird,* which has a related subject.

In 1913 Brancusi's innate elegance was disturbed by the experience of African tribal sculpture. He began to build up his images, as here (fig. 4), by the addition of one cryptic element to another. Vestiges of naturalism remain: Brancusi always started from an exact observation of human idiosyncrasy, and in this case the spindly legs, the slightly turned-in feet and the tall, thin, as yet unrounded torso suggest a particular little girl at a particular stage in her life.

Brancusi was also concerned—along with so many artists at that time—to annex for European art the ferocious energies of so-called "primitive" art.

In the summer of 1910 Margit Pogany sat for Brancusi a number of times (fig. 5). She was a young Hungarian painter studying in Paris, and he especially admired the way in which her head nestled over a strikingly elegant pair of wrists and hands. He went on working from her, or from memories of her, until 1933, and the portraits which resulted are probably the most sustained and celebrated attempt at personification which modern art has to show. Sometimes her huge bulging eyes, her finely drawn nose and her diminutive mouth were portrayed quite naturalistically; sometimes they served primarily to trap the dazzle of light as it fell on an artfully chosen material. Her distinctive and lyrical personality is everywhere present; but sometimes the portrait has the concision of epigram, whereas at other times it appears to us as (to quote Jean Arp—sculptor, poet, pioneer of Dada and Surrealism) "the fairy godmother of abstract sculpture."

4

5. Constantin Brancusi
Mlle. Pogany
(version 1), 1913
The Museum of
Modern Art,
New York

Around the turn of the century Auguste Rodin introduced the idea that a fragmentary sculpture could be exhibited as such, and that its incompleteness might even give it a heightened emotional force. Brancusi was one of the many sculptors—others were Matisse, Boccioni and Duchamp-Villon—who took the hint. In this *Torso* (fig. 6) he reduced the basic facts about the male torso to three gleaming columnar elements. In its rejection of all descriptive or anecdotal matter, and in the candor of its erotic allusion, the work retains, as Sidney Geist has remarked, "a quintessential modernity that must have been the more dazzling when it was created, more than half a century ago."

6. Constantin Brancusi
Torso, 1917
The Cleveland Museum of Art

7. Constantin Brancusi
Bird in Space, 1928?
The Museum of Modern
Art, New York

Brancusi in his many versions of the *Bird in Space* intended to evoke both the effortless upward movement of the bird and the trajectory of its flight (fig. 7). The bird can also be seen as a metaphor for the poetic imagination as it blasts off, unencumbered, into the empyrean.

8. Constantin Brancusi
Fish, 1930
The Museum of Modern Art, New York

Brancusi from 1922 onward tried again and again to make a sculpture which would show not the physical appearance of any given fish but, as he himself said, "the flash of its spirit." Such a sculpture would concentrate on the horizontality of all fish, their slithery and apparently weightless deportment under water, and the smooth and largely featureless nature of their bodies. He tried many materials, many forms of base, many solutions for the problem of how the sculpture itself was to relate to the base. In this particular version he concentrated on the idea of the fish as it lifted itself off the seabed with its mouth tilting ever so slightly upward.

9. Pablo Picasso
Three Dancers Resting, 1925
Private collection, New York

10. Pablo Picasso
Four Dancers, 1925
The Museum of Modern Art, New York

During the period of his active collaboration with Diaghilev, Picasso did not "work from life," as far as the dancers were concerned. But in 1925 he made a number of studies of dancers; he covered the gamut of their day from the most strenuous activity (fig. 10) to moments of repose (fig. 9). At the one extreme he matched the intense physical effort of the dancers with fragmented outlines and significant elongations; at the other, he gave them the timeless look of a relief from ancient Greece.

11. Jean Cocteau
Picasso in 1917 (Parade), 1917
Private collection, England

12. Pablo Picasso
Portrait of Stravinsky, 1917
Private collection, New York

installed it, the collector John Quinn took a great liking to his work, and in 1921 the *Little Review* ran a special Brancusi number with appreciations by Ezra Pound and others. None of this was allowed to interrupt the serene rhythms of Brancusi's working life. He would as soon keep his work as sell it; pieces like the 90-inch-high *Caryatid* stood around in his studio, unremarked and unrecorded, for 40 years; a total immunity to fuss and flummery combined with a streak of peasant cunning to make him the epitome of anti-careerism. Only perfection would do; and if perfection took forever—well, that was quite all right with him.

In the 1920s there was no Apollinaire to act as the nerve center of a pacific International. The masters of the modern movement were moving into middle life; the urgencies of first youth were over. It was too late for a symbiotic alliance of the kind which had united Picasso and Braque until 1914; but effective working partnerships could still be formed, and one of the most fertile of these had been consolidated in Rome in the year 1917 between Pablo Picasso, painter, and Igor Stravinsky, composer. The intermediary in this was Sergei Diaghilev, who had brought his Russian Ballet company to Paris in 1909 and kept it together ever since. Diaghilev had commissioned from Stravinsky the three great ballet scores for which Stravinsky is still best known: *The Firebird, Petrouchka* and *The Rite of Spring;* and Picasso was at that time a camp follower of the company, insofar as he was preparing the scenery and costumes for *Parade,* a ballet first produced in Paris in May, 1917, and was attracted to a member of the company, Olga Koklova, whom he subsequently married.

When they moved on to Naples Picasso and Stravinsky became fascinated by the Commedia dell'arte, a form of street theater which had flourished in Italy for more than three hundred years. One of its main characters, Harlequin, was already a long-time favorite with Picasso and the subject of some of his most deeply felt paintings. But in Naples, where life is lived to a great extent in the street and every man learns in childhood to look after him-

Poet, playwright, novelist, film director and the most famous conversationalist of his time, Jean Cocteau was also a brilliant draftsman (fig. 11). In just a few strokes he could set down, as here, the quintessence of personality. We know, as well as if we had been there ourselves, just how vividly Picasso responded to the sumptuous masquerade of the ballet world.

From 1917 onward Picasso produced a long series of portrait drawings: a private pantheon of the people whom he liked and admired (fig. 12). Pre-eminent among these was the composer Igor Stravinsky.

13. Pablo Picasso
Pierrot, 1918
The Museum of Modern Art, New York

14. Pablo Picasso
Pierrot and Harlequin, 1920
Mrs. Gilbert W. Chapman, New York

self, the most important figure in the Commedia dell'arte was Pulcinella, a hook-nosed, barrel-bodied intriguer with a talent for getting into scrapes and a genius for getting out of them.

PICASSO AND PULCINELLA

Himself no slouch when it came to practical joking, Picasso came to see as much of himself in Pulcinella as he had formerly seen in Harlequin. But although the stock figures of the Commedia dell'arte were in and out of his paintings and drawings throughout 1917 and 1918 the images in question were mostly

Pierrot off duty (fig. 13) was a very different person, in Picasso's mind, from Pierrot on stage (fig. 14). Pierrot off duty, with his mask in his hand and a book open on the table, is manifestly in the real world. He has even an echo of the forlorn performers of Picasso's Rose Period (Volume 2). Pierrot on the stage is quite another matter: a stylized figure who stands head-on to his audience, as if daring them not to give him their full attention.

15. Pablo Picasso
Three Musicians, 1921
Philadelphia Museum of Art

elegiac in tone and had neither the insidious fun nor the potential for horseplay of the Neapolitan performers. Something in the total experience of the Neapolitan street theater had still to come out in Picasso's work; and in December, 1919, with a characteristic flash of inspiration, Diaghilev invited Picasso to join forces with Stravinsky and with the dancer and choreographer Léonide Massine in a ballet to be called *Pulcinella*.

It was difficult in later years to say who had enjoyed *Pulcinella* most: those who devised it, those who appeared in it, or those who just sat there and watched. But for Stravinsky and Picasso it was something more than an immensely successful entertainment which allowed them to quintessentialize a form of theater now extinct.

Stravinsky went so far as to say, in fact, that *Pulcinella* was "the epiphany through which the whole of my late work became pos-

sible." As for Picasso, he used the experience as the raw material for two of the most arresting of 20th-century paintings—the *Three Musicians, I* and *II,* which he painted in Fontainebleau in the summer of 1921. Something more had been at stake, for both of them, than the refashioning on the one hand of songs and instrumental pieces by the 18th-century Neapolitan composer Pergolesi, and the refashioning on the other of costumes long hallowed by tradition.

For Stravinsky, *Pulcinella* meant a decisive shift away from the barbaric energies of his native Russia. It inaugurated the 50 years' investigation of the western European musical tradition which he was to continue in one form or another until the day of his death. There is nothing portentous about the music for *Pulcinella,* and least of all about the formalized ribaldry of the concert suite, which never fails to bring down the house with its buffoonish duet for trombone and double bass; but the decisive shift is there, nonetheless. Equally there are no signs of exceptional involvement in Picasso's working sketches, even if the stocky, belted, great-nosed figure of Pulcinella does have a look of Picasso himself in disguise. But in the one case, as in the other, what had been undertaken as a delightful collaboration, but certainly a task, turned out to have quite another implication.

Pulcinella was first performed in Paris in May, 1920. As late as 1918 Picasso was still preoccupied with Pierrots and Harlequins of a withdrawn and woebegone sort; but from the moment that *Pulcinella* got under way he took a completely new tack. The pictures might be no more than ten inches high, but the figures had the bulk, the aggressivity and the straightforward frontal stance which were needed to win over a difficult audience in the back streets of Naples. Where the *Pierrot* of 1918 (fig. 13) had classical fine features and a look of introspection, the paired figures of 1920 (fig. 14) were as much coded as portrayed. If Picasso wanted to emphasize the hooked nose of Pierrot's mask he would set it firmly in profile, for instance, against the white outline of a head seen from the front; and if Harlequin's right hand was drawn quite realistically, as it hung down from the far side of Pierrot's shoulder, his left one was indicated by four vertical nicks in the baton that Harlequin carried with him everywhere. The paired figures were seen as flat, cut-out giants who filled the whole of the picture space from top to bottom; in this, and in the rhythmic alternations of dark and light which gave vigor and animation to the whole surface of the picture, there were echoes of that most disquieting of earlier Harlequins, the lifesize painting done late in 1915 (Volume 4).

The two versions of the *Three Musicians* (one is now in New York, the other in Philadelphia) are identical in size: more than six feet high, more than seven feet wide (pl. I; fig. 15). They are "lifesize," therefore, with all that that implies in the way of heightened actuality. The three musicians themselves are both in life and apart from it, both real and fictitious. Festive in their costume, they nevertheless bring with them intimations of quite other states of mind. As they face us in their shallow, stagelike space the three musicians echo, for instance, the way in which the Holy Trinity form up in many a Renaissance painting. Equally, they may remind us of the trio of judges—robed, remote and yet with power over life and death—who gaze back at us in Daumier, and later in Rouault. The masker is traditionally a figure both hilarious and sinister. He is the pretender who speaks true. ("The maskers cover their faces," wrote John Lyly in 1580, "that they may open their affections.") By coding his own features the masker could be said to come halfway to meet Cubism. And Cubism, in the *Three Musicians,* comes halfway to meet the maskers, in that they represent between them an anthology of earlier Cubist subject matter: the clarinet, so great a favorite with Braque, the sheet music, the guitar, the sturdy wooden table with its upended top, and (in the Philadelphia version) the hint of a dado. The friar in that same version may remind us also of a famous photograph in which the young Braque is seen sitting down with a concertina on his knee.

Altogether, the two big paintings give us a sense of unfinished business completed once and for all. They have the sleight of hand of a picture like Picasso's *Still Life with Fruit,* 1915 (Volume 4), but with none of that painting's purely decorative aspect; and they have the grave monumental quality of earlier Cubist seated figures without being withdrawn from the hurly-burly of life on stage. They are very witty: note how in the New York version the

16. Georges Rouault
The Three Judges, 1913
The Museum of Modern Art, New York

Rouault had in mind that most pregnant of New Testament sayings: "Judge not, that ye be not judged." And he detested the idea that one man should put on fancy dress to take away another's liberty.

17. Pablo Picasso
Three Women at the Spring, 1921
The Museum of Modern Art, New York

As much as either version of the *Three Musicians* (pl. I; fig. 15), *Three Women at the Spring* belongs to the European tradition of the outright masterpiece. Picasso worked toward it, in Fontainebleau, with what was for him an exceptional slowness and thoroughness, planning and replanning the alignment of the three women, the nature of the background and the extent to which it should be revealed, and the way in which the slow, circling movement of the hands could parallel the slow, circling movement of bared shoulders and bared brows. The final result may also owe something to Fontainebleau itself—its august and ancient artistic tradition, the formal beauty of the Château and its park, even the associations of the name, with its double echo of the French words for "fountain" and "water."

18. Henri Matisse
The Moroccans, 1916
The Museum of Modern
Art, New York

In the winter of 1912–13 Matisse was in Tangier with a French painter called Charles Camoin. Once back in France, he made up his mind to sum up his experience of Tangier in one enormous painting, but it was not until the summer of 1916 that he finally got down to it. It gave him a great deal of trouble. ("I may not be in the trenches," he wrote to Camoin in July, 1916, "but I am in a front line of my own making.") The subject of *The Moroccans* is the terrace of a little café which he and Camoin had frequented in the native quarter of Tangier. Alfred H. Barr's classic analysis of the painting cannot be bettered: "The picture is divided into three sections, separate both as regards composition and subject matter: at the upper left one sees a terrace or balcony with a pot of large blue flowers at the corner, a small mosque beyond and, above, the lattice of a pergola; below, on a pavement, is a pile of four yellow melons with their great green leaves; and at the right are half a dozen Moroccans, one of them seated in the foreground with his back turned, the others, extremely abstract in design, are reclining or crouching with burnouses drawn over their heads. These three groups might be described as compositions of architecture, still life and figures. They are like three movements within a symphony—with well-marked intermissions—or perhaps three choirs of instruments within the orchestra itself."

hands of the cowled figure on the right are sketched in with just two specimens of paper-tearing in the sheet music. And they are minutely thought out: note how in the Philadelphia version Harlequin is not playing a violin, since a violin might not have quite the compositional weight that the picture requires, but the broader-bellied viola.

The two versions differ much more than appears at first sight; and just when we have decided that the New York version is altogether plainer and less "busy" we notice that Picasso has introduced a completely new formal element in the dog which lies beneath the table. Is it a real dog, a rug or a shadow? All three, one could say; and its tail has the further advantage of rhyming with the outline of Harlequin's hat. Fun is never far from the *Three Musicians;* but it does not exclude a most exact and peremptory marshaling of the flat color areas which make up the surface of the picture. In compositional terms the New York version has a severity which, as William Rubin says, "might seem more appropriate to a Byzantine *Maestà* than a group of maskers from the commedia dell'arte; but it is precisely this structuring that informs the monumentality of *Three Musicians* and endows it with a mysterious, otherworldly air."

The *Three Musicians* belongs to the European tradition of the outright masterpiece, in which the artist stands back and sums up what he has lately achieved. Picasso, like Braque, Bonnard and Matisse, had the 19th-century conviction that the duty of the artist was not just to do good work, as part of an ongoing process, but to concentrate his whole energies from time to time on something that could hang in the Louvre with Rembrandt's *Bathsheba* and Poussin's *The Four Seasons* and not be discomfited. The achievement in question was to be deliberate, not accidental; and the process by which it came about was to be fundamentally consolidatory.

When Picasso painted these two pictures that particular ambition was not easily achieved. An aesthetic of immediate astonishment was coming into favor: the after effects of Dada and the current effects of Surrealism were all against the majestic, long-ruminated impact of paintings like these. An art of the here-and-now was coming up over the horizon, whereas the old-style masterpiece matures slowly and can with impunity be put aside for a generation. It was not, for instance, until 1927 that Matisse bestirred himself to show his *The Moroccans* of 1916 (fig. 18) and his *Bathers by a River* of 1916–17 (Volume 6). The dealer Paul Rosenberg bought the New York *Three Musicians* from Picasso in 1921 and kept it by him until 1949. It was not the current form in the 1920s for the major artist to get up in public every year and say, "This is where I'm at."

THE 1920s: A DOUBLE-NATURED DECADE

The 1920s had a double nature. There was the aspect of the decade which has become a part of folk memory. Quick returns and a horror of going on too long are common to many of its manifestations: the cocktail, the wisecrack, the jazz band, the Charleston, the encapsulations of *Time* magazine, the songs of George Gershwin and Noël Coward and Kurt Weill, the contribution of Art Deco to dress and design, the laconic first stories of Ernest Hemingway. Limits were set to scale, to ambition, and above all to the intrusion upon others' time: "An hour is enough of anything," said the American novelist Edith Wharton, one of the most redoubtable hostesses of the day. (A classic of the period is Paul Hindemith's opera *There and Back Again* [1927] in which the action is played twice over, forward and backward, and the audience still gets out in under 20 minutes.)

Folk memory errs, however, in leaving out precisely those vast

and pertinent enterprises for which the 1920s will be longest remembered. If we stick to the conventional view of the decade we may find these ventures anachronistic in their amplitude, foredoomed in the impossible scale of their ambitions, and in more than one case inevitably and predictably unfinished. But we may equally well see them as majestic delaying actions in which were reviewed, almost for the last time, the full resources of the European tradition. Not for them the closed forms and the finite perfection of earlier ages; Ezra Pound made that distinction very clear when he wrote that "art very possibly *ought* to be the supreme achievement, the 'accomplished'; but there is the other satisfactory effect, that of a man hurling himself at an indomitable chaos and yanking and hauling as much of it as possible into some sort of order (or beauty), aware of it both as chaos and potential."

It is exactly this twofold awareness—of an ever-encroaching chaos, on the one hand, and on the other of its unprecedented and unmanageable potential for art—which comes out so strongly in certain voluminous master-works of the 1920s and '30s. Specimens which leap to mind are James Joyce's *Ulysses* (1922), the novel series of Marcel Proust, who died in 1922 with his manuscript still not completely revised; *The Waste Land* (1922) by T. S. Eliot; *The Magic Mountain* (1924) by Thomas Mann; Arnold Schoenberg's unfinished opera *Moses and Aaron* (1930–32); Robert Musil's *The Man without Qualities,* begun in 1930; the *Cantos* of Ezra Pound, begun in 1915 and unfinished even at the time of Pound's death in 1972. There are too many points of kinship between these huge, flawed but still comprehensive summations for us to dismiss the matter as one of coincidence. There is about every one of them something valedictory, as if the end of the recording would signal the end of the thing recorded.

And where did art stand in all this? Betwixt and between. Cubism had been, apart from so much else, a school of concision: no waste, no fat, no rhapsodizing. Insofar as *The Magic Mountain* or *Moses and Aaron* had their equivalents in art, they were in existence already before 1914, in the panoramas of convulsion to which Kandinsky gave the impassive name of Compositions; but when Kandinsky returned to western Europe in the 1920s he turned to a less headlong mode of expression. Paul Klee had, between 1918 and the day of his death in 1940, a delicate and unerring intuition as to what was happening to Europe: but he was not going to launch out on the scale of the Sistine Chapel when he could say all that had to be said on the scale of a pocket handkerchief. Léger had, as we have seen, as keen an eye as anyone for the potential of the 1920s; but when chaos began to get the upper hand of that potential he could offer only a robust irrelevance. (To the end of his days, he believed in the hard-hat as the hope of the world.) The early warning systems of the Surrealists led in more than one case to what can be called a masterpiece. One such was Dali's *Soft Construction with Boiled Beans: Premonition of Civil War,* 1936 (Volume 7), and another Ernst's *The Horde,* 1927 (Volume 7). But the accolade was won involuntarily and in breach, almost, of the Surrealists' charter. (The traditional notion of a masterpiece implied, for one thing, a belief in sober effort.)

On reflection, there could be no doubt that if masterpieces were going to be made in the 1920s and '30s, they would be made in Paris, where the continuum of major art was most strongly in evidence, and made by people brought up in the 19th-century tradition. Who were these people? Matisse, Picasso, Bonnard and Braque. What was so special about Paris? Simply the fact that, as the critic Clement Greenberg said as late as 1946, "Paris remains the fountainhead of modern art. Other places (Berlin at the time of the Weimar Republic, for example) may have shown more sensitivity to immediate history, but it is Paris over the last hundred years that has most faithfully conveyed the historical essence of our civilization." As to the effect of Paris upon those who lived there in the 1920s, James Joyce for one said: "There is an atmosphere of spiritual effort here. No other city is quite like it. It is a racecourse tension. I wake early, often at five o'clock, and start writing at once."

In ways that we recognize but cannot always account for, great art keeps something in reserve for each successive generation. The *Three Musicians* once had a look of pure festivity: but observers from a later generation may be in some doubt as to what would happen if the masks were to be laid down. We know more today about the function of role-playing in human affairs. We may have seen Jean Genet's play *The Balcony* (1956), in which a false judge, a false general and a false bishop act out the roles which their costumes impose upon them. What if Picasso's harlequinade should be headed for a sinister ending? We shall never know the answer, but there is something minatory about the *Three Musicians* which plays directly on the nerves of a generation which was not even born when it was painted.

In formal terms, some of the works which we are considering here are sedate by comparison with their predecessors in the heroic period. But a particular weight and assurance may turn out to reside in that very steadiness, that specific air of acquiescence in procedures which were already a part of history. I can best demonstrate this by examining two paintings which Picasso completed in the spring and summer, respectively, of 1925. They could not be less alike. *The Three Dancers* (pl. III) speaks for a

19. Jean Baptiste Siméon Chardin
Attributes of the Arts, 1765
Musée du Louvre, Paris

Chardin's casual-seeming composition conceals a whole complex of allusions: to the notion of fame, to the painter's brushes and the sculptor's hammer, to the raw material of still life (which Chardin himself had invested with a new dignity), to geometry the mother of perspective, and to the gold or silver coins which could stand either for History encapsulated or for the artist's amply justified earnings.

grief that is violent, destructive and disorderly. *Studio with Plaster Head* (pl. II) is outstanding for its vivacity, its contrapuntal control and its wide range of perfectly adjusted allusion. *The Three Dancers* could be called the last masterpiece of European Expressionism, just as the *Studio with Plaster Head* could be related to the French still-life tradition. Both readings would be correct. Expressionism—the use, that is to say, of distortion in the interests of a greater intensity of feeling—can show nothing more telling than the strange antics, halfway to hysteria, which unite Picasso's dancers. The order, the balance, the sense of organization that characterize French still life in the 17th and 18th centuries find their consummation in the *Studio with Plaster Head,* where Picasso includes several of the properties most favored by Chardin when he painted his *Attributes of the Arts*: a plaster cast from the antique, a scroll of drawing paper, a geometrical instrument and a book (fig. 19).

Yet how much is still unsaid! The *Three Dancers* represents, in a context of private desolation, a number of motifs that we associate with a civilized well-being: the patterned wallpaper familiar from Cézanne onward, the tall window open to a southern sea, the unflawed blue of the sky, and the shaped energies of the dance. The subject of the picture is the transformation of this scene by the intrusion of grief in its most extravagant and implacable form. The picture was prompted by the death of a Spanish friend of Picasso's, a fellow painter who had been close to him in his youth; the dead man's profile can be seen beneath the left arm of the central figure in the painting. Picasso was not the man to render grief in terms of genteel resignation. His instinct was rather—in the words of Dylan Thomas's lines to his father—to "rage, rage against the dying of the light." But by the time that the picture was bought for the Tate Gallery in London in 1965, history had caught up with it on two important counts. One of these was first identified by André Malraux in 1947 in *Museum without Walls*, volume 1 of his book *The Psychology of Art*. André Malraux was then at the height of his fame as a novelist, as a resistance leader, and as potentially one of the most important men in a resuscitated France. His stature as a philosopher of history has been called in question since then; but there has been the most widespread practical assent, even among those who have never heard his name, to the basic idea of the *Museum without Walls*, which is that we are no longer tied to any one style as representative of our age, but are free to anthologize as seems to us best. Malraux made, in 1947, his own personal anthology among the art works of the past; in doing so he authorized for the general public a practice which had been common form among men of genius for the best part of half a century.

In the 1920s and '30s words like "eclectic" and "opportunistic" had been used of the foreign language quotations which bring *The Waste Land* to a close, and of Stravinsky's use of the Latin language—"a medium not dead," he said, "but turned to stone"—in *Oedipus Rex*; it was common form, equally, to speak of Picasso's borrowings from the past in terms of pure pastiche. But in time it became clear that what was important in such borrowings, whether by Eliot or Stravinsky or Picasso, was the degree of their reinvention. Something about the left-hand figure in *The Three Dancers* was mysterious to many people when the picture first came to London; then the art historian Lawrence Gowing identified her as a derivative of the Maenad as Bacchante, a motif first known to us in Greek reliefs and later taken up by Donatello when he grouped the three Marys at the foot of the cross. The Maenad in question was a dancing figure who had a tambourine crooked under her right arm. Picasso had a great deal of trouble to get her right; but, as Gowing says, "the figure that emerged was the same figure that had been drawn from antiquity five hundred years earlier for the same purpose. . . . It was recreated in

The Three Dancers to fill the same need, to epitomize the agonizing incongruity between death and sensual life, which is the source of grief."

History had also caught up with *The Three Dancers* by the late 1960s insofar as we had had continual reminders from news photography of the way in which people react in real life to unexpected and appalling situations. In the light of such reminders the left-hand figure in Picasso's painting is not at all histrionic in her bodily contortions, in the disorder of her dress, or in the grimace which tears her face in two. This is what grief does to people. We had seen it in art before—in Gothic sculpture, for instance, where the sculptor spares us nothing of the physical impact of mourning—but before we could *feel* it again someone had to reinterpret it.

To say the last word about a great painting is always a vain endeavour; it will look different, in any case, to those who come after us. *The Three Dancers* is about the dance, but the dance seen as convulsion. It is about the crucifixion image—a tall thin figure with upstretched arms, outlined against a T-shaped cross. It is about mourning and about the aggressivity, the wish to take Destiny by the throat, to which mourning notoriously gives rise. It is about Cubism, and about the way in which Cubism can operate within a complex system of allusion. And it is about the painter's job, part of which is to bear witness to the worst that can happen to human beings.

The *Studio with Plaster Head* at first sight seems much less complex in its implications. Its subject matter is surely straightforward enough—the table itself (cut foursquare to steady the composition); the tumbled cloth, a triangular fold of which reappears beneath the table to balance the many triangular forms in the upper half of the canvas; the insistent, repeated pattern of the wallpaper; the mass-produced woodwork, here given a most powerful thrust and counter-thrust; the Chardinesque group of evocative objects. The only thing that speaks loud and clear for the 1920s is, in fact, the toy theater—a precise rendering of a recent gift from Picasso to his four-year-old son—which makes us wonder if we are indoors or out-of-doors as we explore the top left quarter of the painting. (Even the sky looks like a painted sky and seems to be both outside the window and inside the theater.)

A tour de force, therefore, of ingenuity and high spirits: a working model of a world in which reality and make-believe change places and nothing can ever go wrong. But something more than that, as well. Those severed arms and hands, for instance, and the big sculptured head which we see three times (in shadow, in profile and in a half-hidden frontal view): are they

II. Pablo Picasso
Studio with Plaster Head, 1925
The Museum of Modern Art, New York

14

III. Pablo Picasso
The Three Dancers, 1925
The Tate Gallery, London

20. Henri Matisse
Nude Study, 1907
The Museum of Modern Art, New York

Back I, 1909

Back II, 1913

21. Henri Matisse
Series of four reliefs
The Museum of Modern Art, New York

Back III, 1916–17

Back IV, 1930

Matisse was interested in the idea of the relief made flesh: the standing woman pressed against a wall, in other words, in such a way that she and the wall become one. He made a powerful drawing of the subject (fig. 20) and over the next 21 years he made a series of over life-sized reliefs on the same theme (fig. 21). In pursuing this one subject with such persistence, Matisse certainly had in mind the dream, common to many gifted artists before 1914, of a truly monumental sculpture. He may have had in mind, also, the pungent phrasing of Rodin, who said that sculptors should not shirk the challenge of the spine, considered as "the principal armature, the very equilibrium of the human body." He certainly remembered the look of the women's backs in the Cézanne which he himself owned (Volume 2). Sometimes the Backs series ran parallel with a major painting, as when number *III* took up an idea that occurs also in the *Bathers by a River* of 1916–17 (Volume 6). Sometimes a Back had a premonitory importance, as when number *IV* foreshadowed the radical simplifications of the cut-paper figures of the 1950s. (Matisse had the plaster of number *IV* in his studio at that time and looked at it every day.) Whether or not he meant them to be shown as a series, the Backs relate over and over again to his deepest preoccupations.

just decorative additions to an already crowded scene? Certainly the hand meant enough to Picasso for him to remake it on its own many years later, in sculpture, and with an effect of peculiar poignancy. And what about that sprig of laurel, soon to wither? Picasso in the summer of 1925 was living quietly in a still unspoiled Juan-les-Pins, and as he was not at all a political person nothing is less likely than that he consciously foresaw the downfall of Europe. But there is in great art a clairvoyance for which we have not yet found a name, and still less an explanation; and there is no doubt that in the *Studio with Plaster Head* Picasso was making ready the language which he would need both for *Guernica*, 1937 (fig. 55), and for the expression of more private exasperations in years to come. More exactly, as William Rubin has pointed out, the look of the plaster head in the painting of 1925 forecasts the rictus of dismay which we see on the severed head of the soldier in *Guernica*. And the severed arm reappears, holding a broken spear, in that same formidable picture. The *Studio with Plaster Head* looks brisk enough, open enough, pellucid enough; but it runs a gamut of experience that ranges from civilized recreation (reading, drawing, the stage) to pre-echoes of *The Charnel House* of 1944–45 (Volume 1). Faced with paintings such as this, which can be thought over for a lifetime, it is more than ever difficult to see the 1920s as a period of secondary achievement in art.

If the 1920s have that reputation it is because the best work of the period so often turns up in isolation, with none of the armature of chronology with which we can find our way, week by week, through the heroic age of modernism. Even the best artists have dry periods: no one can make history every day of his life. A long patience and a strategy of withdrawal or concealment may be the best way of coping with these periods. The great Europeans with whom we are dealing were prepared to lie low, or to shift their ground, or to withhold all news of their activity in ways that would now be taken as evidence of instability or decay. They were forgetful, too: Matisse did not even remember whether there were three pieces or four in the series of Backs (fig. 21) which was fundamental to his activity as a sculptor. Everything would come out, sooner or later; meanwhile there was the day's work to be got on with.

BONNARD FROM START TO FINISH

A case in point is that of Pierre Bonnard. For reasons which have never ceased to be valid, Bonnard gets away to a very good start in the history books. From 1888 he was part of the new painting as it was being formulated under the influence of Gauguin. He knew the new novelists, the new composers and the new poets. He sat in on rehearsals at the Théâtre de l'Oeuvre, at that time the most adventurous theater in Europe. He was admired by Félix Fénéon, the most discerning critic of the day, and he was taken up by Ambroise Vollard, who for all his half-awake ways was in a class by himself as a dealer. It is difficult, as we have seen, to find a comment on human affairs that is stronger or more candid than Bonnard's *A Man and a Woman*, 1900 (Volume 2).

Then two things happened. One was that Bonnard found himself walled up alive with the woman who shared his life from 1894 onward and eventually, in 1925, became his wife. When Bonnard first met her, she was only 16 and had the quality, irresistible at that time, of a lost child; the 1890s were the heyday of Maeterlinck's *Pelléas et Mélisande*, and Bonnard may well have felt that he had come upon Marthe as Golaud, in act 1, scene 1 of the play, comes upon Mélisande. But as she grew older Marthe Bonnard came to have a horror of society, and Bonnard for a great part of his life was compelled to live quite alone with her. Old friends were unwelcome, new ones unthinkable; the sociable, quick-witted Bonnard of the 1890s dropped out of sight.

It also happened that Bonnard and his friend Vuillard were no longer in the foreground of the modern movement. Other people and other ways were talked about from 1905 onward with a vivacity and a commitment which were not in evidence when Bonnard showed, year by year, at the Bernheim-Jeune gallery. Bonnard went to all the galleries and he looked carefully at the Fauve paintings in 1905, and the first Cubist paintings in 1908, and the pasted-papers of Picasso and Braque in 1913. He particularly liked the way the collaged parts of the pasted-papers introduce an element of physical reality which heightens our awareness of the parts that are drawn or painted. But his personal contacts at that time were with older artists: Claude Monet, who lived not far from Bonnard's house in the Seine Valley, and Auguste Renoir, whom he saw constantly when wintering in the south of France; and it bothered him to foresee—quite rightly—that people would think of him primarily as a belated Impressionist: someone who came along when the real work had already been done.

"We were left hanging in the air," Bonnard said later of the situation of himself and his friends in 1914. "We had wanted to take the same direction as the Impressionists, but to go further than they did in the rendering of color as it actually exists in Nature. But art and Nature are two different things. . . . And then progress came upon us faster than anyone expected, and the public was ready for Cubism, and even for Surrealism, before we had realized our intentions completely."

22. Pierre Bonnard
Evening in Paris, 1911
The Hermitage Museum, Leningrad

Bonnard as a young man was in and out of the theater all the time; and in the Parisian scenes which were bought before 1914 by a discerning Russian collector there were elements of theater in the lateral, friezelike presentation, in the choice of groups and attitudes that would make their point instantaneously, and in the quick-witted delineation of individual character. Bonnard here is like a photographer who can work with a hand-held camera and exposure of 1/100th of a second when everyone else is still stuck with the equipment of a generation earlier.

It was in these circumstances that Bonnard went back to school, as he himself put it, and tried to combine the unmistakable Bonnard-note with a more formal architecture and a more radical use of color. By 1928, when Bonnard painted *Le Café du Petit Poucet* (pl. IV) for his friend the art critic George Besson, pure abstract painting in its sterner, more mathematical guise was familiar to anyone who kept in touch with current developments in art. Bonnard did not go along with this, but he knew that as early as 1916–17 Matisse had partitioned his *Bathers by a River* with vertical lines that imposed a strict, steady, left-to-right progression upon it. And when Bonnard came to paint the Besson picture he imposed upon it, likewise, a series of vertical divisions. These were owed in literal terms to the architecture of the café; but in combination with the horizontal lines of the awning, and of the glassed-in area on the left of the canvas, they gave the picture a geometrical structure which was quite lacking from such pre-1914 paintings by Bonnard as the *Evening in Paris* of 1911

(fig. 22). In 1911 Bonnard was at the height of his graphic period: he wrote into his pictures whatever happened to amuse him in Parisian street life, and relied on color to bind the composition together. That color, though unmistakably his, was careful—anchored, one might say, to a preexisting system. Seventeen years later the graphic gift was no less in evidence: not even in the novels of Colette, at her best, do we get a clearer idea of how people in Paris dressed, sat, crossed the street or walked into a café in the year 1928. Even the red and yellow piping on the backs of the café chairs is exactly right. But Bonnard in 1911 would not have secured so precise, and yet so apparently casual, a series of shallow curves as the one that begins in the foreground with the hooped back of the wicker sofa, moves on through the hooped backs of the wicker chairs and carries among the ovals of the cloche hats which were then mandatory among Parisian ladies. Nor would he have stiffened the composition with the precisely drawn rectangles which stand for the lighted windows across the street; these remind us that for all its amusing social detail this painting has also its mathematical side.

"A picture," Bonnard said, "must be a little world sufficient unto itself." With the green of fresh almonds, with an orangey yellow, and with the deep violet that stood midway between them, he had his way with Nature. Tyrannizing his subject matter, bending space to his will, he in later life allowed himself a total liberty where color was concerned. And when it seemed likely that all this would result in something luscious but formless, daring but fundamentally illegible, it turned out that Bonnard had remembered the lessons not only of the "advanced" painting of his own day but of a master not usually mentioned in this context: Vermeer.

Bonnard had, pinned up in his studio, a postcard of Vermeer's *The Little Street* (fig. 25). It might have seemed irrelevant to his own work; but if we look closely at a masterpiece of Bonnard's middle 60s, the *Nude in Bathroom,* 1932 (pl. VI), certain shared preoccupations will appear. Vermeer's *Street* is remarkable for the ingenuity with which he has patterned almost the entire surface of the canvas with rectangles of one kind or another: the brickwork, the lattice of the windows, the doorways, the shutters (both open and closed), the cut of the benches on the street, the deeply indented roof. Vermeer also included in the upper left-hand area some contrasted diagonals; and all this gives a particular poignancy and an unforced naturalness to the figures of the four human beings, young or old, as they go about their business. We realize, finally, that there is something unexpectedly modern about the way in which Vermeer has parceled out the picture surface and conferred upon almost two-thirds of it a

IV. Pierre Bonnard
Le Café du Petit Poucet, 1928
Musée des Beaux-Arts, Besançon (France)

24. Pierre Bonnard
Boulevard des Batignolles, 1926
Private collection, Switzerland

25. Jan Vermeer
The Little Street, c. 1658
Rijksmuseum, Amsterdam

Bonnard was, with his friend Edouard Vuillard, the last great painter to portray a Paris not yet ruined by the automobile.

literal flatness: one backed up, that is to say, by the nature of the things portrayed.

Bonnard's picture is set, as were so many of his later paintings, in the bathroom in which his wife spent a disproportionately large amount of her time. Like the Vermeer it has been given a tectonic quality by the division of a great part of the canvas into rectangles, large or small. The vertical lines of table, window-frame and what looks to be a curtain are balanced by the fat blue line which runs across the canvas between the edge of the tiled floor and the foot of the wall. All this brings out the flatness of the picture surface in ways not often equalled since Matisse, in 1911, would organize almost the whole of a picture in terms of a continuous repeated arabesque on an uninflected red ground and yet make the whole scene read quite clearly (*The Red Studio,* Volume 2).

23. Pierre Bonnard
Nude in Bath, c. 1935
Honorable Walter H. Annenberg, Philadelphia

In the heyday of Surrealism Bonnard was often written off as an earthbound artisan, over-concerned with subjects that by their very nature were sedate and repetitious. But in pictures like the *Nude in Bath,* Bonnard showed qualities of daring and invention which make most of the Surrealists' fancies look both

labored and gratuitous. In the reinvention of color he goes far beyond the Fauves. In the use of multiple viewpoints he makes most Cubist painting look dull and regimented. He also introduces an element of psychological ambiguity which is neither forced nor over-explicit. The picture contradicts all our expectations. Who else would have made the far end of the bath look like the blank wall of a reservoir, or contrasted the demure, lace-ridden figure on the left with a pair of legs that look as if they might have come straight from a slaughterhouse?

Where Bonnard went beyond Matisse was in his entirely arbitrary use of color—switching tiles from blue and white to yellow and white, for instance, and getting his planes to overlap and intermingle, clear at one point and opaque at another, in ways that are nearer to Synthetic Cubism than to Impressionism. Like Vermeer, he introduced a diagonal, just below the slatted shutter. This prevented the composition from getting too stiff (it also balances the parting in Madame Bonnard's hair). And, again like Vermeer, he gave the human figure an unaffectedly touching and vulnerable look by setting off its rounded forms and air of preoccupation against the rigorous marshaling of flat forms in all the rest of the picture. Bonnard did, on the other hand, take liberties with the human body which would never have occurred to Vermeer: the forward movement of his wife's right leg in the *Nude in Bathroom* could have been painted only by someone who had seen how Cézanne, in his *Grandes Baigneuses* (Volume 1), had let feeling take precedence over exactitude. In this inexhaustible picture the dog is a survivor from the world of Manet's *Olympia* (Volume 1), where it was taken for granted that every pretty woman had an animal of some sort as witness to the secret rituals of beauty. As for Marthe Bonnard herself, Bonnard was too chivalrous to monitor the inevitable decay of the compact little body which he had recorded so often and, at the outset, so faithfully. I suspect, in fact, that he drew upon the memory of that antique marble whose photograph was pinned up on the studio wall beside the Vermeer.

Bonnard in this painting borrows from the antique world not only the forms of the body, but also the sacrificial manner in which Madame Bonnard addresses herself to what is in itself quite a commonplace action. There is something in this of that backward glance toward happier days which we find in the marble grave reliefs which proliferated in ancient Greece after the end of the Peloponnesian War. It was in just such terms that the Greeks commemorated the dead mistress of the house at a time of national misgiving. I have suggested that in the 1920s and early '30s the arts in Europe had in common a wish to re-examine the achievements of the past in ways which might yield strength where strength was much needed. If we accept that idea, there can be included among the rewards of this great and complex painting an echo of that earlier time when art had "kept its calm even in the midst of catastrophe."

All this takes us a long way from the Bonnard whose landscapes and still lifes can be read in terms of pure seduction. But then Bonnard is not the only major artist who is too often associated primarily with the amiabilities of life. Matisse for many years was regarded as not quite serious, on the basis of those

26. Pierre Bonnard
The Worktable, 1926–30
Mr. and Mrs. Paul Mellon, Washington, D.C.

As Bonnard moved through middle age, something of the incisive wit of his first youth fell away from his art. But in *The Worktable* the cat and the dog are as sharply characterized as they would have been in the 1890s; as for the sonorous rug that loops its way through the bottom half of the painting, Bonnard may have had it in mind to rival Matisse in his mastery of patterns that in lesser hands would have wrecked the whole picture.

V. Pierre Bonnard
The Breakfast Room, c. 1930–31
The Museum of Modern Art, New York

VI. Pierre Bonnard
Nude in Bathroom, 1932
The Museum of Modern Art, New York

MATISSE AT FULL STRETCH

27. Albert Marquet
Two Friends, 1912
Musée des Beaux-Arts, Besançon (France)

Quiet and unassuming in his ways, Albert Marquet was somewhat put upon by his old friend and classmate Matisse. (After one visit from Matisse, he said, "I felt like a curate when the Bishop comes to tea.") But in *Two Friends,* he touched on an aspect of the life of the emotions which Matisse would never have treated so directly. Whereas in a Matisse like *The Moorish Screen* (pl. VII) we stand back and admire some elegant play acting, in *Two Friends* we eavesdrop upon a genuine human involvement.

many paintings from his years in Nice which appeared to ignore both the chaos of which Ezra Pound wrote and, more especially, its potential for art. It was at the cost of a continual struggle, both with the subject matter and with himself, that he painted pictures like *The Moorish Screen,* 1922 (pl. VII), but it was a matter of pride with him to conceal that struggle from the public. The end result was curiously neutral, in emotional terms, as if the people portrayed had come to exist only as captives of Matisse's will. The work was perfect, within its own terms: no one has ever reordered the world with greater dexterity. But something of human involvement was lost—as we may see if we compare *The Moorish Screen* with the picture called *Two Friends* which Matisse's close friend Albert Marquet painted in 1912 (fig. 27).

Matisse between 1918 and 1925 was like a sundial that marks only the unclouded hours. There is a most evident contrast, for example, between the gaunt confrontation of *The Painter and His Model* in 1917 (fig. 33) and the Nice version (1919) of the same subject (fig. 28). But this was not because Matisse had gone soft. It was because he was applying the pressure elsewhere. Not many people know, even today, the strenuous little sculptures with which Matisse came to terms in 1918–19 with quite another side of his nature. In the Nice *Artist and His Model* of 1919, we glimpse the long slender brush with which Matisse, in a distillation of delight, would feather his subject matter from the overcrowded little room onto the canvas. The sculptures come from something quite different: what the art historian Albert Elsen has called "the desire to shape and feel the literal fullness of a woman's body." Matisse was furthered in that desire by close study both of Michelangelo (in particular the famous figure of *Night* in the Medici Chapel in Florence) and of antique sculpture. Like Bonnard, he responded to the beauty and poignancy of those young female torsos that have come down to us from the Hellenistic world. In fact he owned a Roman copy of a Greek torso of the 4th century B.C.; and whereas in his paintings and drawings of the 1920s he allowed himself merely to dominate the naked female figure from a distance he took quite a different liberty when sculpting in private and on the scale of his everintrusive thumb. His tiny *Torso* of 1929 (fig. 30) makes visible one of the most insistent of masculine daydreams: that the phallus should become one with the body that it has penetrated.

Matisse was a man of many guises. Unsurpassed as the poet laureate of indolence, he also kept into old age the ability to tackle a completely new task, no matter how arduous it might be. Timing played a great part in this: for Matisse knew just when to stay where he was and when to cut and run. His decisions were predicated in part on the wish to retain his powers in their totality until extreme old age. But there also entered into them something that has now vanished: a belief in serious European art as a continuum. "An artist of talent cannot do what he pleases," he said in 1936. "We are not the masters of what we produce. It is imposed upon us." Matisse saw himself as part of an organic process in which his role, as a gifted individual, was to remain alert to what needed to be done at any given time.

In this context, Matisse also saw himself—and quite rightly—as the complete artist: the man who could do anything. He could paint, he could sculpt, he could draw, he could make prints, he could illustrate on the grand scale, he could design scenery and

28. Henri Matisse
Artist and His Model, 1919
Mr. and Mrs. Harry Bakwin, New York

29. Henri Matisse
Seated Nude, 1925
The Baltimore Museum of Art

30. Henri
Matisse
Small Torso,
1929
Private
collection

31. Henri Matisse
Seated Nude with Arms Raised, 1925
The Museum of Modern Art, New York

In April, 1918, Matisse became preoccupied with Michelangelo's figure of
Night in the Medici Chapel in Florence. Over the next six years that heavy-
limbed and melancholic sculpture continued to haunt him; and in 1924 he
transposed it, in Parisian terms, into a lithograph entitled *Night*. The notion of
a seated woman with her arms raised and one knee drawn high above the
other had a fascination for him which remained intact even when all direct
echoes of Michelangelo had been left behind and the emotional climate was
one of a benevolent neutrality (fig. 31). But when Matisse made his definitive
attack on the subject in sculpture (fig. 29), he abandoned the pulpy, easy-going
fleshy quality of the lithograph and drew with the knife, as it were. In this
way he imparted a drumlike tension at both the chest and the belly and took
away every hint of flabbiness about the legs. The woman in the lithograph
needs the chair at her back, both physically and psychologically; the woman in
the sculpture could hold her pose forever, so trim and taut is her figure, so
all-pervading the sense of energy balanced and held in equilibrium.

VII. Henri Matisse
The Moorish Screen, 1922
Philadelphia Museum of Art

32. Henri Matisse
Studio, Quai St. Michel, 1916
The Phillips Collection, Washington, D.C.

Matisse in earlier years (see *The Red Studio* of 1911, Volume 2) had seen his studio as a sanctuary and a treasure house. But the years 1916–17 were crucial to the survival of France as a free nation, and something of the times got into these paintings. In the earlier of the two, the studio is a mixture of condemned cell and operating theater: all is bare, sparse, severe (not least, the house fronts across the Seine and the staircase that leads down from the bridge to the quayside), and the painter himself is not even present. In the second, the baroque looking-glass and the classic Parisian balcony rail alone relieve the plainness of the scene; and the artist is seen as a kind of generalized bolster, engaged on a task that drains away his individuality as a social being. It is one of the lessons of this painting that art demands the whole self: nothing less will do.

33. Henri Matisse
The Painter and His Model, 1917
Musée National d'Art Moderne, Paris

34. Georges Braque
The Mantelpiece, 1922
The Museum of Modern Art, New York

35. Pablo Picasso
Guitar over Fireplace, 1915
The Museum of Modern Art,
New York

36. Henri Matisse
The Window, 1916
The Detroit Institute of Arts

costumes for the stage. At every turn he was conscious of the European tradition which lay behind him. There was no reason to suppose that that tradition would be interrupted, or that artists of comparable accomplishment would not go on feeling that Matisse was in back of them, just as the Greeks, the Italians of the Renaissance, the Dutch painters of the 17th century, and the unfaltering relay team of the French School had been in back of Matisse since he first picked up his brushes in 1890.

He did not, however, see the limits of art as having been established once and for all. Himself the author of some of the most covetable of all easel paintings, he was nonetheless convinced that "one day easel painting will cease to exist. Things are changing all round us, and eventually mural painting will take over." When easel painting gave him only intermittent satisfaction, as was the case in the 1920s and '30s, he would embark on a series of prints, a long meditated construct. It was as if he carried within himself not only the past of European art, but its future as well; and never more so than in the enormous commission which he completed in 1930–33 for the Barnes Foundation in Pennsylvania.

Matisse knew that the only department in which modern art had yet to excel was that of the alliance between painting and architecture. The modern movement had reached its highest point in the self-sufficing, autonomous, portable statement. Only once or twice had a Rousseau, a Kandinsky, a Bonnard, a Léger or a Delaunay worked on the scale which Tintoretto and Rubens had taken for granted. Matisse with *Dance* and *Music* in 1909–10 (Volume 2) had a chance of that sort; and now, in 1930, he had it again.

It was not an easy task. Dr. Albert C. Barnes, the Argyrol millionaire, had built in Merion, a suburb of Philadelphia, a sizable

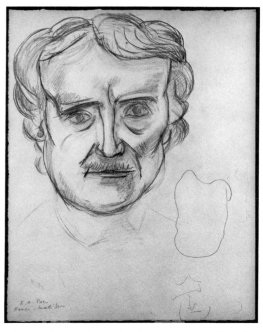

37. Henry Matisse
E. A. Poe, 1931–32
The Baltimore Museum
of Art

When making etchings for the poems of Mallarmé in 1931–32, Matisse seized with particular enthusiasm on Mallarmé's tribute to Edgar Allan Poe. Like many another eminent Frenchman, he ranked Poe very high; and he devised for his portrait a harassed but all-seeing gaze which sums up both the anguish and the great good fortune of the predestined poet.

Picasso and Matisse, Braque and Bonnard were never allies, in the sense that Picasso and Braque were allies before 1914; but ideas passed from one to the other, back and forth and irresistibly, to the day of their deaths. Picasso in 1915 had the idea of the mantelpiece—tall, flat, with a shelf at the top—as an ideal subject for paintings that would combine elements of architecture with elements of still life (fig. 35). After his demobilization from the army Braque was to take up this idea and bring to it (fig. 34) an unmatched command of texture and a stately grandeur of tone. Matisse in 1916 used that staple ingredient of French interior decoration, the splay-footed table, as the animating feature of *The Window* (fig. 36); in a composition where so much depends on tall straight vertical lines, he used the feet of the table to persuade us to circle round from one part of the picture to another. Just such a splay-footed table was to be taken up by Braque a decade later; and Braque made something special of the symphonic interior in which magic was made from a standard French middle-class living room.

mansion in the French style with stone brought from château country in the center of France. This he had filled with a collection primarily of French 19th-century painting, in which Cézanne, Seurat, Renoir and Matisse himself predominated. The room which Matisse was to decorate was already hung with easel paintings of such quality that, as Matisse said himself, "another painting would simply have been out of place." Extending above the masterpieces in question was a row of windows, each 18 feet high, which looked out onto tall trees. Higher still were the three lunettes, nearly 12 feet in height at their highest point and in all nearly 16 yards across, which Matisse was to fill as he thought best. Between these lunettes were two pendentives which came down so low that the visitor has almost to bend double, in his imagination, to get from one lunette to the next. Three self-contained images would have filled the space acceptably; but Matisse was determined to overcome the awkwardness of the site. He wanted a dynamic image; one that would make the visitor

29

forget that in relation to the room as a whole the lunettes were just three dumpy little spaces between the windows and the roof.

Most of the terms of Matisse's contract with himself were negative, therefore. The mural was not to be "another painting": there was to be no rivalry with the easel pictures below. The mural also had to stand up for itself at two completely different levels. From the floor it was to function as a substitute for the sky, which could not be seen through the windows. But from the balcony level, to which every visitor climbs in the course of his visit, the mural had to read as a statement on its own. A double play

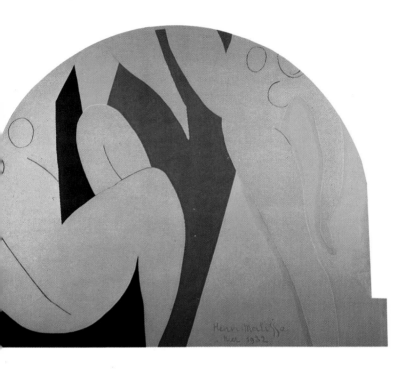

VIII. Henri Matisse
Dance I, 1931–32
Musée d'Art Moderne de la Ville de Paris

38. (*below left*) Henri Matisse
Dance II, 1932–33
Copyright 1974 by The Barnes Foundation, Merion, Pa.

of perspective was added, in this way, to problems which were already thorny enough. Matisse also took due account both of the color of the stone and of the fact that the only source of light was from below.

In his preliminary sketches Matisse made use of his recent sculptural experience to produce group after group of athletic Amazons, each one superbly realized in the round and set against the dense and vibrant color which Matisse had perfected during his many years at the easel. But they were rejected, in turn, when Matisse found that they were forming up *as pictures* and not as an integrated mural. What he made in the end was fundamentally a huge drawing, carried out by himself with the help of a long pole. So far from giving in to the stunted conditions which were imposed by the architecture, Matisse presented his figures as giantesses who were far too tall to fit into the threefold frame. This allowed him to generate a degree of physical excitement which takes the visitor by surprise. It is as if the stone had spawned human figures many times larger than life and was no longer able to restrain them.

Not everyone can get to see the Barnes mural, and it has never been reproduced in color. So it remains one of the more secret

of this century's enterprises. (Matisse did it twice over, in point of fact, since Dr. Barnes gave him the wrong dimensions the first time round; the earlier version [pl. VIII] is now in the Musée d'Art Moderne de la Ville de Paris.) The mural is important not only for itself but because Matisse pioneered in it a notion which was of great importance to art after World War II: that of the painting as arena, and of the final result as something owed to a physical encounter between the painter and a given number of square feet of space. If Matisse was "born to simplify painting," as his teacher had told him in the 1890s, this was one of the ways in which he passed on his mandate to posterity. He was to do it to even more spectacular effect at the very end of his life in big cut-paper decorations where painting was dematerialized and color was as near as not made incorporeal. Meanwhile the Barnes mural set an august precedent.

THE STRATEGIES OF BRAQUE

Matisse went on renewing himself, even into the 1950s, by finding new solutions for new tasks. This was never the case with Braque. Everything that Braque did in middle and later life turned out in the end to be a way of nursing painting along; and as he

31

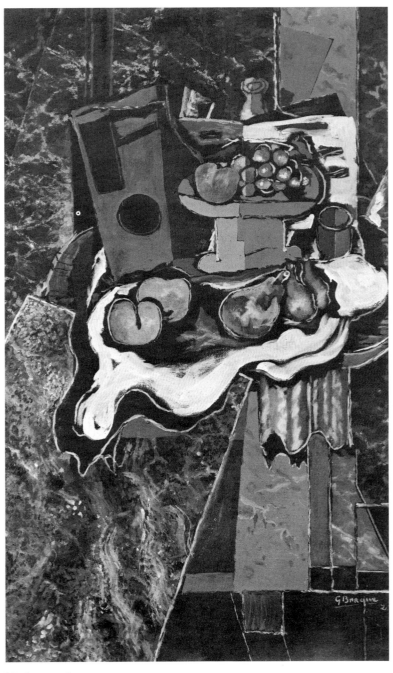

39. Georges Braque
Still Life on a Marble Table, 1925
Musée National d'Art Moderne, Paris

grew older and frailer his studio became the whole world for him and he reacted hardly or not at all to the outside involvements—exhibitions, major commissions, polemics in print—on which art history battens. He painted for himself, not for the historian. Interpretation of his work seemed to him at best superfluous, at worst actively harmful. "The only valid thing in art is the one thing that cannot be explained," he once wrote; and in the 1950s he said that "to explain away the mystery of a great painting would do irreparable harm, for whenever you explain or define something you substitute the explanation or the definition for the real thing."

It takes a rash man to ignore a warning of that sort. But it ought to be said that these remarks apply above all to Braque's paintings of the 1940s and '50s, in which he went all out for what he called a metamorphic ambiguity; in other words, he blurred the distinction between the real and the imaginary, the literal and the metaphorical, the named and the unnamed. In those late paintings identities melt like butter in the pan; where ambiguity is fundamental to the picture it is reasonable enough that the artist should resent any attempt to explain it away. Even in a relatively early painting like the *Café-Bar* of 1919 (Volume 4) there are passages where the images overlap in such a way that we are hard put to disentangle them. Braque at that time prepared his canvases with what the art critic John Richardson calls "a thickish sandy layer of matt black paint, which [Braque] compared to coffee grounds or tea leaves because, like a fortune teller, 'he can divine there things which others cannot see.'" This dense black foundation conferred upon his images a kind of immunity: press them too hard to declare their identity and they vanish.

But, like the other great Frenchmen of his generation, Braque was a strategist. It was not at all his style to peak in his 20s or 30s and thereafter go into a long decline. He was also anxious to nurse painting, as I said earlier, through a difficult period in its evolution. What Léger aimed to do by close attention to the Aviation show, and what Matisse hoped to do by a sage diversification of his activities, Braque did by staying still in one place and counting up the things that he could do better than anyone else. He had the true French feeling for continuity; he would never have talked as Arnold Schoenberg talked when he said to a visitor in 1922 that he had "discovered something that will guarantee the supremacy of German music for the next one hundred years," but he did undoubtedly intend to put French painting beyond the reach of rivalry.

He had, to begin with, an unequaled sense of touch. No painter has put on canvas a more varied or a more consistently delectable substance than Braque. Next, he had a sense of the space

40. Georges Braque
The Black Rose, 1927
Mr. and Mrs. Burton Tremaine, Meriden, Conn.

41. Georges Braque
Vase, Palette and Skull, 1939
Mr. and Mrs. David Lloyd Kreeger, Washington, D.C.

in his paintings as being infinitely adjustable: something that could be bent back, folded over, hinged, cut into slivers and made transparent or opaque as suited him best. In particular, he learned to maximize the impact of his sense of touch by bringing the objects in his still lifes within reach, one and all. He carried over from Synthetic Cubism the practice of distributing color without regard for its local allegiances, and he felt at liberty to reorder the shapes of things in the interests of a majestic harmony of his own devising.

All this went in tandem, throughout his career, with a total appreciation of the still uncorrupted countryside of France, and of the things which it could produce for the still-life table top. Looking at a picture like his *The Black Rose,* 1927 (fig. 40), we remember what the Goncourt brothers said of Chardin: that he could reproduce for us "the shaggy velvet of the peach, the amber transparency of the white grape, the sugary rime of the plum, the moist crimson of strawberries, the hardy berry of the muscatel and its smoke-blue film, the wrinkles and tubercles of an orange skin, the embroidered guipure of melons and the copperas of old apples. . . ." But when we look more closely it turns out that what Braque sets before us is an equivalent, not an imitation; in this context Braque evokes, but does not specify.

When ruminating on the nature of art, and on the tasks which art could still validly undertake, Braque was at one with Matisse and Picasso in that he turned again and again to the studio itself for his subject matter. The best way to think about art was to see what actually happened when someone was making it. The act

of painting was a metaphor for creativity in its purest, most absolute form, and a lot of irrelevance could be avoided if the scrutinies of art were turned inward, upon art itself; that was the idea, and it lent itself to the widest possible range of statement. Picasso in the late 1920s most often took an aggressive and schematic point of view, emphasizing the polarization of artist and sitter and the ways in which the information given by the sitter's appearance is censored (or added to, or transformed) by the time it reaches the canvas. Matisse enjoyed playing with our expectations in such a way that we are never for instance quite sure (as in *The Artist and His Model,* 1936; fig. 46), whether we are looking out of a window onto a real landscape or whether we are looking at a picture that has been hung on the wall in just the right place. (In this case it's a picture: a cartoon for a tapestry in which Matisse drew on his memories of a visit to Tahiti.) Braque

IX. Georges Braque
Le Guéridon (The Round Table), 1929
The Phillips Collection, Washington, D.C.

In this, one of the grandest and most
completely realized paintings of our century, Braque summed up once and for all
the traditional preoccupations of Cubism:
the splay-footed table with its arcaded
support, the piece of sheet music, the
pipe, the musical instrument, the labeled
bottle, the scrolled dado, the still life of
fruit. He also introduced the knife which
from Edouard Manet onward had been an
important element in still life. And at the
top of the canvas, where the convergence
of walls and ceiling can make for dullness,
he brought the whole matter down to
within an inch or two of the observer's
nose and animated it with shifts of
perspective and changes of color.

X. Georges Braque
Studio Interior with Black Vase, 1938
Mr. and Mrs. David Lloyd Kreeger, Washington, D.C.

As he grew older, Braque began to pit the identities of art against the identities of everyday life. In a painting like this everything has equal status: the paneled wall, the grained wood of the easel, the vivid wallpaper, the palette with dabs of paint still wet, the canvas on the easel and the framed canvas on the wall. Braque practiced, as between each and every one of these surfaces, a perfect equality: none had precedence over the others. Each form, each plane, each texture, each nicely contrasted patch of color slid into its place.

43. Henri Matisse
Reclining Nude in Studio, 1935
Mr. and Mrs. Nathan L. Halpern, New York

42. Henri Matisse
*Artist and Model Reflected in
a Mirror,* 1937
The Baltimore Museum of Art

44. Pablo Picasso
Page from the Vollard suite
of etchings

45. Henri Matisse
*The Painting
Lesson,* 1919
Scottish National
Gallery of
Modern Art,
Edinburgh

46. Henri Maisse
*The Artist and His
Model,* 1936
Mr. and Mrs.
Ira D. Wallach,
New York

In the etchings which he produced for publication by Ambroise Vollard, Picasso returned over and over again to the theme of the artist, his model and the work of art which was to result from their meeting. The severe schematic researches of 1927–28 were often replaced—as here—by a relaxed and quietly ribald comment on the human comedy as it manifests itself in the production of art.

In contrast to the full-scale confrontations on canvas in which the relationship of the artist and model was explored in the 1920s and '30s by Picasso, by Braque, and by himself, Matisse in the mid-1930s made a series of pen and ink drawings where the same subject was treated with a free-running and mischievous fancy. Sometimes, as in fig. 42, the naked figure of the model was seen twice over, while the artist himself, upright and formally dressed, was glimpsed at work in the background. At other times, as in fig. 43, Matisse not only repeated the image of the model in a mirror but referred more than once to his own activity. We see the model; we see the model reflected in the mirror; we see the sheet of paper on which she is being represented; and we see an echo of the sheet itself, with the artist's hand busy at its work. (Even the thumbtack on the drawing board has its echo.) Matisse delighted in these feats of virtuosity and prided himself on making them look the easiest and most natural thing in the world.

The move to Nice was fundamental to Matisse's development. The South of France was still unspoilt at that time and Matisse just couldn't believe that the sunshine, the vivid light from the sea, the flowers fresh from the market and the endless supply of pretty and amiable models were his for the asking, day after delectable day. A great change came over his work. Every least detail of his subject matter took on a festive look, from the palm tree which kept finding its way into the pictures to the stripes on the painter's own pajamas. The set-faced verticals of 1916–17 were replaced in *The Painting Lesson* by that most relaxed of shapes, the oval laid on its side. Painting was no longer a matter of life and death; yet in the *Artist and His Model* (fig. 46) there is energy to spare in the virtuosity with which portrait is played off against still life, indoors against outdoors, and pattern against texture.

36

47. Pablo Picasso
Painter and Model, 1928
The Museum of Modern Art, New York

Picasso could keep a dozen ideas going at a time. In *Painter and Model* he showed his awareness of Matisse in the patterning (white on yellow) of the painter's chair in the lower right-hand corner. He remembered the ferocious reworking of the human face in Oceanic art when it came to his presentation both of the painter's own face and of the face of his model. Reversing the traditional procedures of modern art, he metamorphosed the head of the model into a naturalistic profile on the canvas. He also remembered the decorative flat patterning of Art Deco (then at its height) when he came to organize the picture in terms of interlocking flat planes. These planes rhymed with the natural flatness of the chair back, the chair's tasseled fringe, the picture on the wall, the wall itself, and the stylized dado which traverses the wall at shoulder height. The use of bright flat color relates, also, to current practice in architecture (see, for this, the workings of De Stijl; Volume 8).

did not align himself with either, but went quietly ahead with his own inquiries, which were about the extent to which objects can lose their identities and yet retain them. He wanted to find out how many different kinds of reality could live together within a single picture and in ways that only painting could bring about.

All this took him a long way from the Cubism of 1910–12, which was fundamentally an art of plain statement about a small number of identifiable facts. But Braque in the 1930s was a very different person from the enormously strong young man who before 1914 could overturn a carnival float with his own two shoulders. There is in great art an element of historical fatality; but something is also owed to the private evolution of an individual human being. Braque's health never recovered from the wounds which he sustained in 1915, and in middle life he had none of the power of attack which made Picasso react instantaneously to whatever happened around him. ''A picture is not a snapshot,'' Braque said in 1939; and in the late 1930s he began to treat the world in terms of a consciousness which took as much account

48. Henri Matisse
Papeete (or *Window on Tahiti*), 1935
Private collection, New York

XI. Georges Braque
The Billiard Table, 1949
Mr. and Mrs. Leigh B. Block, Chicago

In the Cubism of 1909–14 our knowledge of objects is assembled in a new way; old sums yield new results; what had been hidden is brought into view. In Braque's late paintings the element of accountancy is still there, in the hat on its rack in the upper left corner and the criss-cross tiling on the floor. But by 1949 he had moved into a world in which words like "solid" and "trans-parent," "near" and "far," "real" and "unreal" have no meaning. In life, a billiard table is a rectangle, faired and squared to the nearest millimeter; in this painting it is hinged, tilted up and toward us, and turned into an irregular six-sided object. From somewhere behind it, Braque releases a squadron of intruders with wings outstretched. As with the bird on the easel in figure 50 we cannot tell whether they are real birds, or birds painted on a hanging behind the billiard table, or a mixture of both. But, whatever they are, they invest this complex and supremely beautiful painting with an aerial mystery and a sense of incorporeal wonder which can be found nowhere else in modern art.

49. Georges Braque
Still Life: The Table, 1928
National Gallery of Art, Washington, D.C.

of what was not as of what *was*. He was still interested in fact, and was as ready as ever to evoke a specific kind of graining in wood or the precise outline of a bottom-heavy jug. But if mystery entered into his experience—if there was a bird on the canvas on the easel, for instance, and if that bird seemed to take off and fly around the room—Braque did not demur. Nor did it at all disturb him if objects came adrift from their presumed positions in space and floated around the room in a state of transparency. This vision of a world in a state of perpetual flux, motion and change was, after all, no more unreal than the traditional

picture image of a world artificially stilled and categorized according to a single unvarying canon.

These are philosophical paintings, therefore, even if the manner of their presentation is irresistibly voluptuous. Such a gamut of sanded tans, so close a conjunction of purple and violet had rarely been seen before. As surely as the Surrealists, but with none of their sensational or pathological subject matter, Braque in the 1930s reintroduced the irrational into painting. (In 1935 he said that "writing a poem, painting a picture, carving a stone—all three of them are irrational acts.") What he wanted at that

50. Georges Braque
Studio (with Wooden Stool), 1939
Lucille Simon, Los Angeles

51. Georges Braque
Still Life, 1938
Mr. and Mrs. Leigh B. Block, Chicago

As in Picasso's *Painter and Model* of 1928 (fig. 47), the studio itself is represented mainly in terms of tall flat rectangular panels. But Braque allowed himself an infinitely greater license in the matter of textures, in the scale on which individual objects are presented and in the way in which space is reordered. Objects move forward and back, turn opaque or transparent, at the painter's whim. Real flowers are set off against simulated ones; imitation wood is set off against the real thing. As with the splay-footed table in Matisse's *The Window* of 1916 (fig. 36), the spokelike interweaving of the seat of the stool on the right is used to guide us gently from one point of the compass to the next. As for the bird on the easel, it is the forerunner of many others in Braque's later work (see plate XI). Is it a picture of a bird? Or is it a real bird that has flown into the studio from outside and is posing in front of the easel? Or is it a painted bird that has "chosen liberty" and refused to stay on the canvas? Braque isn't telling: this is just the kind of poetic ambiguity which he most enjoyed.

time was to achieve an equipoise, peculiar to himself, between logic and the free play of instinct—and between the strict scaffolding of Cubism as it had evolved before 1914 and the fluidity and irrationality of life as it actually presents itself.

It could be argued from 1933 onward that philosophical inquiry might well be suspended, in deference to the steadily worsening condition of Europe. Braque did not agree. "We must insist," he said in 1939, "on a categorical distinction between act and actuality." This belief has sometimes got him into trouble with self-appointed moralists, most of whom have never seen a shot fired in anger, let alone fought as gallantly as Braque. Where the future of Europe was concerned Braque saw as clearly, and felt as deeply, as any other intelligent and humane observer. But in his art he was an armored man, and the pictures went their own way without interruption until France herself was brought almost to a standstill during the later stages of the German occupation.

Throughout the 1930s Braque was free, moreover, to wall himself up in his studio, if he so wished. The case was very different for Paul Klee, who in 1933 was deprived of the right to teach in Germany and in 1934 learned that the Nazis had ordered the confiscation of a book on his work which had been written by his old friend Will Grohmann. Switzerland was the country of Klee's birth, and to that extent his misfortunes were mitigated; but he felt them acutely, nonetheless, and his son Felix has described how one of his first actions on arriving in Switzerland as a refugee was to make a little picture called *Struck Off the List.* Klee was sensitive to every vibration of the world around him—after the outbreak of World War I in 1914 he wrote in his diary, "For a long time I have carried this war within me"—and between 1933 and

52. Paul Klee
Letter Ghost, 1937
The Museum of
Modern Art,
New York

Waiting for a letter that does not come is torture. What could be more natural, to Klee's way of thinking, than that letters should have ghosts—white-faced presences that take on the look of a human head and a pair of shoulders?

53. Paul Klee
Imprisoned Animal, 1940
Private collection, Switzerland

Klee did not apply himself in literal terms to the history of his own times. But we know, all the same, that this imprisoned animal with its huge staring eyes is a metaphor for the millions of people who were to experience imprisonment in one form or another in the 1940s.

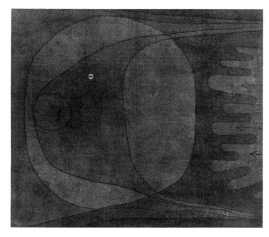

54. Paul Klee
Fear (Angst), 1934
The Museum of
Modern Art,
New York

Klee saw fear in terms of an inescapable intrusion. In this oblique but unforgettable image, it is as if a man were trying to escape from his terrors in sleep, only to find that fear has impregnated the very blankets which he tries to pull up to his chin.

his death in June, 1940, he referred over and over again in his work to the all-encompassing persecution which was the lot of so many of his friends and colleagues.

He never did this in a literal or a descriptive way. It was not his role to duplicate what could be seen on the newsreels or read about in those newspapers which could still report freely. He was there to find what he had so often found before in happier contexts: the perfect metaphor for what everyone was feeling but no one knew as well as he how to express. He set before us the idea of fear, at a time when virtually every European had fear as his daily companion. He imagined his *Letter Ghost* (fig. 52) at a time when not to get a letter often meant the arrest, if not the death, of the person who had gone to the mailbox as a free hu-

man being the week before. The image of an imprisoned animal in 1940 (fig. 53) was as poignant to Klee, and therefore to ourselves, as was the image of the imprisoned unicorn to the people who made *The Hunt of the Unicorn* tapestries in the 15th century. It is thanks to people like him, as much as to commentators of a more straightforward kind, that posterity knows what it was like to live in Europe at that time.

Yet there is certainly a case for saying that in terms of immediate public impact Picasso's *Guernica* was a greater service to humanity, at the time it was painted, than any other single painting of its date. It was in April, 1937, that the Spanish city of Guernica was destroyed by German aircraft under the order of General Franco. The world has seen many such things since, and

XII. Pablo Picasso
Interior with Girl Drawing, 1935
Private collection, New York

As on other occasions, Picasso here combines themes of his own invention with memories of Matisse. The act of drawing, as in itself a subject for a drawing or painting, had preoccupied him for years. He was close enough to the Surrealists to know how important was the role, in their activity, of automatic writing. The dream, as epitomized by a beautiful girl with her eyes shut, had been a favorite subject of his for several years. In the present painting these ideas are combined with the relaxed state of mind of Matisse's *The Painting Lesson* of 16 years earlier (fig. 45), with its absorbed figure on the right-hand side of the canvas, its slender vase filled with flowers, and its allusion on the left-hand side of the canvas to the end-product to which all art is directed.

55. Pablo Picasso
Guernica, 1937
The Museum of Modern Art, New York

seen them on a bigger scale and with more calamitous weapons. But at the time there was something uniquely chilling about the deliberate obliteration of a historic city. Six days later Picasso began work on the huge monochromatic painting which bears the name *Guernica.* This painting was shown from July, 1937, onward in the Spanish Pavilion at the Paris International Exhibition; and as a contribution to the poetics of outrage it made a colossal effect.

GUERNICA AS POLEMIC

It is a tribute to the power of *Guernica*—and a comment, also, on the confusion of the times—that we still find it difficult to place the picture, once and for all, in the context of Picasso's output. He himself said in 1965 that as between *Guernica* and *The Three Dancers* of 1925, "I much prefer *The Three Dancers.* It's more a real painting—a painting in itself without any outside considerations." And there is in *Guernica* something descrip-

tive—something of the "Agit-prop" wall-newspaper raised to the scale of epic—which lays it open to comprehensive explanation in just the way that Braque regarded as unworthy of high art. But there are moments in history at which it is more important to strike hard and strike soon than to aim at the privileged status of high art, and the summer of 1937 was one of them.

In painting *Guernica* Picasso took up a challenge—that of the specific event from recent history—which for one reason and another is now often regarded as being outside the province of serious art. Its affinities in that respect are with the 19th century: with Goya's *The Third of May, 1808,* Delacroix's *Liberty Leading the People,* Manet's *The Execution of the Emperor Maximilian.* Beyond these it looked back to a classic figure subject from still earlier days—the Massacre of the Innocents. At the same time it has characteristics which relate it to our own era: the image is put before us in the blacks and whites of the 1930s newsreel, and the scale and format foreshadow the sprawling animation of the

56. Pablo Picasso
Still Life with Red Bull's Head, 1938
The Museum of Modern Art, New York

wide-screen movies of the 1960s. There is something of everything in *Guernica,* from the tabloid headline to distant echoes of 11th-century Spanish illuminated manuscripts. On one level the imagery is as explicit as that of a news photograph; on another it secretes layer upon layer of recondite allusion, some of it conscious, some of it most probably not.

There are in existence 45 preliminary studies for *Guernica,* all but one of them dated. There are also seven photographs of successive phases during the painting of the picture itself. We know a great deal about *Guernica,* therefore. We know that the figure of the wounded horse derives from a drawing made by Picasso in 1917, and that the striped skirt and flung-back head of the woman on the left derive from the mourning Maenad in *The Three Dancers* of 1925. The broken spear and the head of the dead soldier in *Guernica* hark back, as we also know, to the *Studio with Plaster Head,* again of 1925. There are many pre-echoes in Picasso's work for the figure of the bull, bemused and stationary despite all the tumult around him. If the arm that holds the lamp seems to be 15 feet long, and if the necks of the four women seem to be made of elastic, these elongations were initiated in the 1920s, when Picasso spent a lot of time at the seaside

and noticed how people seem to deny their normal dimensions when they get to run and jump around the beach.

Every great artist carries much of the past of art within him, and when he is under exceptional pressure the past is likely to break in, unbidden, in ways not to be foreseen. When the English art historian Anthony Blunt published a book on *Guernica* in 1969 he had no difficulty in tracing the formalized masks of Picasso's women to massacre subjects painted in the 17th century by Guido Reni and Nicolas Poussin. But along with identifiable borrowings of this kind there came allusions of an oblique and perhaps involuntary sort. On the ground in the middle of the picture, beneath the forefeet of the horse, there is for instance a flower for which no logical reason can be adduced in a purely metropolitan scene. "Is it permissible," Blunt asks, "to see in this an allusion to the anemone which sprang from the blood of Adonis and became a symbol of his resurrection?"

Guernica is, therefore, on one level a polemical painting that goes all out for quick results. On another, it stands for that general mobilization of the European past which was art's last line of defense in the 1920s and '30s. It can be seen as a magniloquent patchwork, and it can also be seen as one of the instances in which a major modern artist has faced directly up to his responsibilities as a social being. As to precisely where the truth lies, opinions are likely to vary from one age to another. My own view is that as larger lunacies efface the memory of the destruction of Guernica, the picture is likely to look more and more like an isolated phenomenon in Picasso's work: one that by the standards of the highest art relies too much, as Picasso himself said, on "outside considerations." It stands out, all right; but does it quite stand up? Does it do something that could not be done in any other medium, or is there in the end too much of illustration in it?

When Picasso painted his *Still Life with Red Bull's Head* (fig. 56) in November, 1938, he must have had this problem on his mind. For what he did was to carry over from *Guernica* the steady flame which stands for reason and truth; with it, he carried over the head of the bull. Between the two are a palette and a book, symbols of the power to make truth visible. There are changes, since *Guernica.* Not only has the bull's head been skinned, but it has taken on an unmistakable look of Picasso himself. The huge helpless head glares across at the flame; the painter's tools lie to hand; the picture has a message: it is that it is one thing to see the truth and quite another to know how to put it on canvas. Nothing in this picture is explicit; but like so much that we have considered here it is a delaying action on behalf of a European tradition far gone in decline.

SUGGESTED READINGS

General

Malraux, André. *The Psychology of Art.*
    New York, Pantheon Books, 1949.

Malraux, André. *Museum without Walls.* (Vol. 1 of *The Psychology of Art.*)
    Garden City, N.Y., Doubleday, 1963.

Pierre Bonnard

Fermigier, André. *Bonnard.*
    New York, Abrams, 1969.

Terrasse, Antoine. *Bonnard.* (Taste of Our Time ser.)
    Geneva, Skira, 1964.

Constantin Brancusi

Geist, Sidney. *Brancusi. A Study of the Sculpture.*
    New York, Grossman, 1968.

Giedion-Welcker, Carola. *Constantin Brancusi.*
    Basel, Benno Schwabe; New York, distributed by Wittenborn, 1959.

Jianou, Ionel. *Brancusi.*
    New York, Tudor, 1963.

Spear, Athena T. *Brancusi's Birds.* Catalogue raisonné.
    New York, New York University Press, for the College Art Association of America, 1969.

Georges Braque

Mullins, Edwin. *The Art of Georges Braque.*
    New York, Abrams, 1968.

Ponge, Francis, Descargues, Pierre, and Malraux, André.
    Georges Braque. New York, Abrams, 1971.

Richardson, John. *Georges Braque.*
    Greenwich, Conn., New York Graphic Society, 1961.

Russell, John. *Georges Braque.*
    London, Phaidon, 1959.

Cooper, Douglas. *Braque: The Great Years.* Catalogue.
    Chicago, The Art Institute of Chicago, 1972.

Sergei Diaghilev

Buckle, Richard. *Costumes and Curtains from the Diaghilev and de Basil Ballets.*
    New York, Viking, 1972.

Kochno, Boris. *Diaghilev and the Ballets Russes.*
    New York, Harper and Row, 1970.

Percival, John. *World of Diaghilev.*
    New York, Dutton, 1971.

Paul Klee

Grohmann, Will. *Paul Klee.* First publ. 1954.
    New York, Abrams, 1966.

Haftmann, Werner. *The Inward Vision: Watercolors, Drawings, Writings.*
    New York, Abrams, 1958.

Klee, Felix. *Paul Klee: His Life and Work in Documents.*
    Selected Posthumous Writings and Unpublished Letters.
    New York, Braziller, 1962.

Klee, Paul. *The Diaries of Paul Klee, 1898–1918.*
    Klee, Felix, ed. Berkeley, University of California Press, 1964.

Henri Matisse

Barr, Alfred H., Jr. *Matisse: His Art and His Public.*
    Reprint. First publ. 1951.
    New York, The Museum of Modern Art, 1974.

Flam, Jack D. *Matisse on Art.*
    London, Phaidon, 1973.

Elsen, Albert E. *The Sculpture of Henri Matisse.*
    New York, Abrams, 1972.

Moulin, Raoul Jean. *Henri Matisse: Drawings and Paper Cut-Outs.*
    London, Thames and Hudson, 1969.

Russell, John. *The World of Matisse, 1869–1954.*
    (Time-Life Library of Art.)
    New York, Time-Life, 1969.

Pablo Picasso

Ashton, Dore. *Picasso on Art: A Selection of Views.*
    (Documents of 20th-Century Art ser.)
    New York, Viking, 1972.

Barr, Alfred H., Jr. *Picasso: Fifty Years of His Art.* Reprint. First publ. 1946.
    New York, The Museum of Modern Art, 1974.

Blunt, Anthony. *Picasso's "Guernica."*
    New York, Oxford University Press, 1969.

Brassaï, Jules Halasz. *Picasso and Company.*
    Garden City, N.Y., Doubleday, 1966.

Leymarie, Jean. *Picasso: The Artist of the Century.*
    New York, Viking, 1972.

Rubin, William. *Picasso in the Collection of The Museum of Modern Art.*
    New York, The Museum of Modern Art, 1972.

Penrose, Roland. *Portrait of Picasso.*
    2nd rev. and enl. edition.
    New York, The Museum of Modern Art, 1971.

LIST OF ILLUSTRATIONS

Dimensions: height precedes width; another dimension, depth, is given for sculptures and constructions where relevant. Foreign titles are in English, except in cases where the title does not translate or is better known in its original form. Asterisked titles indicate works reproduced in color.

Bonnard, Pierre
(1867–1947)

Evening in Paris, 1911 (fig. 22)
Oil on canvas, 30¼ x 49 inches
The Hermitage Museum, Leningrad

Boulevard des Batignolles, 1926 (fig. 24)
Oil on canvas, 25 x 26 inches
Private collection, Switzerland

The Worktable, 1926–30 (fig. 26)
Oil on canvas, 48 x 36 inches
Mr. and Mrs. Paul Mellon, Washington, D.C.

Le Café du Petit Poucet, 1928 (pl. IV)
Oil on canvas, 52¾ x 80¼ inches
Musée des Beaux-Arts, Besançon (France)

The Breakfast Room, c. 1930–31 (pl. V)
Oil on canvas, 62⅞ x 44⅞ inches
The Museum of Modern Art, New York
Given anonymously

Nude in Bathroom, 1932 (pl. VI)
Oil on canvas, 47½ x 46¼ inches
The Museum of Modern Art, New York
Extended loan of the Florene May Schoenborn
    and Samuel A. Marx Collection

Nude in Bath, c. 1935 (fig. 23)
Oil on canvas, 40 x 25 inches
Honorable Walter H. Annenberg, Philadelphia

Brancusi, Constantin
(1876–1957)

Magic Bird (Pasarea Maiastra), version 1, 1910
    (fig. 2)
White marble, 22 inches high; limestone pedestal,
    in three sections, 70 inches high
    (the middle section is the *Double Caryatid*)
The Museum of Modern Art, New York
Katharine S. Dreier Bequest

The Kiss, c. 1912 (fig. 1)
Limestone, 23 x 13 x 10 inches
Philadelphia Museum of Art
The Louise and Walter Arensberg Collection

Mlle. Pogany, version 1, 1913 (fig. 5)
Bronze (after a marble of 1912), 17¼ inches high
The Museum of Modern Art, New York
Acquired through the Lillie P. Bliss Bequest

The First Step, 1913? (fig. 3)
Crayon, 32⅜ x 15 inches
The Museum of Modern Art, New York
Benjamin Scharps and David Scharps Fund

Figure (Little French Girl), 1914–18? (fig. 4)
Wood, 49 x 8¾ x 8½ inches
The Solomon R. Guggenheim Museum, New York

Torso, 1917 (fig. 6)
Brass, 18⅜ x 12 x 6⅝ inches
The Cleveland Museum of Art
Hinman B. Hurlbut Collection

Bird in Space, 1928? (fig. 7)
Bronze, 54 inches high
The Museum of Modern Art, New York
Given anonymously

Fish, 1930 (fig. 8)
Marble, 21 x 71 inches
The Museum of Modern Art, New York
Acquired through the Lillie P. Bliss Bequest

Braque, Georges
(1882–1963)

The Mantelpiece, 1922 (fig. 34)
Oil on canvas, 51¼ x 29¼ inches
The Museum of Modern Art, New York
Extended loan of the Florene May Schoenborn
    and Samuel A. Marx Collection

Still Life on a Marble Table, 1925 (fig. 39)
Oil on canvas, 52 x 29½ inches
Musée National d'Art Moderne, Paris

The Black Rose, 1927 (fig. 40)
Oil on canvas, 20 x 37 inches
Mr. and Mrs. Burton Tremaine, Meriden, Conn.

Still Life: The Table, 1928 (fig. 49)
Oil on canvas, 32 x 51½ inches
National Gallery of Art, Washington, D.C.
Chester Dale Collection

Le Guéridon (The Round Table), 1929 (pl. IX)
Oil on canvas, 58 x 45 inches
The Phillips Collection, Washington, D.C.

Still Life, 1938 (fig. 51)
Oil on canvas, 45½ x 58¼ inches
Mr. and Mrs. Leigh B. Block, Chicago

Studio Interior with Black Vase, 1938 (pl. X)
Oil and sand on canvas, 38¼ x 51 inches
Mr. and Mrs. David Lloyd Kreeger,
    Washington, D.C.

Vase, Palette and Skull, 1939 (fig. 41)
Oil and sand on canvas, 36⅛ x 36¼ inches
Mr. and Mrs. David Lloyd Kreeger,
    Washington, D.C.

Studio (with Wooden Stool), 1939 (fig. 50)
Oil on canvas, 45½ x 58¼ inches
Lucille Simon, Los Angeles

The Billiard Table, 1949 (pl. XI)
Oil on canvas, 58 x 78 inches
Mr. and Mrs. Leigh B. Block, Chicago

Chardin, Jean Baptiste Siméon
(1699–1779)

Attributes of the Arts, 1765 (fig. 19)
Oil on canvas, 36¼ x 58 inches
Musée du Louvre, Paris

Cocteau, Jean
(1889–1963)

Picasso in 1917 (Parade), 1917 (fig. 11)
Drawing
Private collection, England

Klee, Paul
(1879–1940)

Fear (Angst), 1934 (fig. 54)
Oil on burlap, 20 x 21⅞ inches
The Museum of Modern Art, New York
Gift of Nelson A. Rockefeller

Letter Ghost, 1937 (fig. 52)
Gouache, watercolor and ink on newspaper,
    13 x 19¼ inches
The Museum of Modern Art, New York
Purchase

Imprisoned Animal, 1940 (fig. 53)
Gouache on paper, 12¼ x 19¼ inches
Private collection, Switzerland

Marquet, Albert
(1875–1947)

Two Friends, 1912 (fig. 27)
Oil on canvas, 23¾ x 36¼ inches
Musée des Beaux-Arts, Besançon (France)

Matisse, Henri
(1869–1954)

Nude Study, 1907 (fig. 20)
Pen and ink, 10½ x 8⅝ inches
The Museum of Modern Art, New York
Carol Buttenwieser Loeb Memorial Fund

Back I, 1909 (fig. 21)
Bronze relief, 74⅜ x 44½ x 6½ inches
Back II, 1913
Bronze relief, 74¼ x 47⅝ x 6 inches
Back III, 1916–17
Bronze relief, 74½ x 44 x 6 inches
Back IV, 1930
Bronze relief, 74 x 44¼ x 6 inches
The Museum of Modern Art, New York
Mrs. Simon Guggenheim Fund

The Moroccans, 1916 (fig. 18)
Oil on canvas, 5 feet 11⅜ inches x 9 feet 2 inches
The Museum of Modern Art, New York

The Window, 1916 (fig. 36)
Oil on canvas, 57½ x 46 inches
The Detroit Institute of Arts
Gift of Mrs. George Kamperman in memory of her husband, Dr. Kamperman

Studio, Quai St. Michel, 1916 (fig. 32)
Oil on canvas, 57½ x 45¾ inches
The Phillips Collection, Washington, D.C.

The Painter and His Model, 1917 (fig. 33)
Oil on canvas, 57⅞ x 38¼ inches
Musée National d'Art Moderne, Paris

The Painting Lesson, 1919 (fig. 45)
Oil on canvas, 29½ x 37 inches
Scottish National Gallery of Modern Art, Edinburgh

Artist and His Model, 1919 (fig. 28)
Oil on canvas, 25⅝ x 28¾ inches
Mr. and Mrs. Harry Bakwin, New York

* *The Moorish Screen*, 1922 (pl. VII)
Oil on canvas, 36¼ x 29¼ inches
Philadelphia Museum of Art
Bequest of Lisa Norris Elkins

Seated Nude with Arms Raised, 1925 (fig. 31)
Lithograph, 25⅛ x 18⅞ inches
The Museum of Modern Art, New York
Abby Aldrich Rockefeller Fund

Seated Nude, 1925 (fig. 29)
Bronze, 30¾ inches high
The Baltimore Museum of Art
The Cone Collection

Small Torso, 1929 (fig. 30)
Bronze, 3 inches high
Private collection

E. A. Poe, 1931–32 (fig. 37)
Pencil, 13 x 10⅛ inches
The Baltimore Museum of Art
The Cone Collection

* *Dance I*, 1931–32 (pl. VIII)
Oil on canvas, 11 feet 8½ inches x 42 feet 1 inch
Musée d'Art Moderne de la Ville de Paris

Dance II, 1932–33 (fig. 38)
Oil, 11 feet 8½ inches x approximately 47 feet
Copyright 1974 by The Barnes Foundation, Merion, Pa.

Papeete (or *Window on Tahiti*), 1933 (fig. 48)
Tapestry: silk and wool, 88 x 68 inches
Private collection, New York

Reclining Nude in Studio, 1935 (fig. 43)
Pen and ink, 17¾ x 22⅜ inches
Mr. and Mrs. Nathan L. Halpern, New York

The Artist and His Model, 1936 (fig. 46)
Oil on canvas, 32¼ x 24 inches
Mr. and Mrs. Ira D. Wallach, New York

Artist and Model Reflected in a Mirror, 1937 (fig. 42)
Pen and ink, 24⅛ x 16 1/16 inches
The Baltimore Museum of Art
The Cone Collection

Picasso, Pablo
(1881–1973)

Guitar over Fireplace, 1915 (fig. 35)
Oil, sand and paper on canvas, 51¼ x 38¼ inches
The Museum of Modern Art, New York
Extended loan of the Florene May Schoenborn and Samuel A. Marx Collection

Portrait of Stravinsky, 1917 (fig. 12)
Pencil, 10 x 18 inches
Private collection, New York
Photograph: courtesy of Richard L. Feigen and Co., New York

Pierrot, 1918 (fig. 13)
Oil on cardboard, 36½ x 28¾ inches
The Museum of Modern Art, New York
Sam A. Lewisohn Bequest

Pierrot and Harlequin, 1920 (fig. 14)
Gouache, 10¼ x 8 inches sight
Mrs. Gilbert W. Chapman, New York

* *Three Musicians*, 1921 (pl. I)
Oil on canvas, 79 x 87¾ inches
The Museum of Modern Art, New York
Mrs. Simon Guggenheim Fund

Three Musicians, 1921 (fig. 15)
Oil on canvas, 80 x 74 inches
Philadelphia Museum of Art
The A. E. Gallatin Collection

Three Women at the Spring, 1921 (fig. 17)
Oil on canvas, 80¼ x 87¾ inches
The Museum of Modern Art, New York
Mr. and Mrs. Allan D. Emil, 1952

* *The Three Dancers*, 1925 (pl. III)
Oil on canvas, 84¾ x 56 inches
The Tate Gallery, London

Three Dancers Resting, 1925 (fig. 9)
Ink on blue paper, 14 x 10 inches
Private collection, New York

Four Dancers, 1925 (fig. 10)
Pen and ink, 13⅞ x 10 inches
The Museum of Modern Art, New York
Gift of Abby Aldrich Rockefeller

* *Studio with Plaster Head*, 1925 (pl. II)
Oil on canvas, 38⅝ x 51⅝ inches
The Museum of Modern Art, New York
Purchase

Painter and Model, 1928 (fig. 47)
Oil on canvas, 51⅛ x 64¼ inches
The Museum of Modern Art, New York
The Sidney and Harriet Janis Collection

* *Interior with Girl Drawing*, 1935 (pl. XII)
Oil on canvas, 51⅛ x 76⅝ inches
Private collection, New York

Guernica, 1937 (fig. 55)
Oil on canvas, 11 feet 6 inches x 25 feet 8 inches
The Museum of Modern Art, New York
Lent by the artist

Still Life with Red Bull's Head, 1938 (fig. 56)
Oil on canvas, 38⅛ x 51 inches
The Museum of Modern Art, New York
Promised gift of Mr. and Mrs. William A. Burden,
  New York

Page from *Picasso for Vollard* (fig. 44)
From original etching
Published by Harry N. Abrams, New York, 1956

Rouault, Georges
(1871–1958)

The Three Judges, 1913 (fig. 16)
Gouache and oil on cardboard, 29⅞ x 41⅝ inches
The Museum of Modern Art, New York
Sam A. Lewisohn Bequest

Vermeer, Jan
(1632–75)

The Little Street, c. 1658 (fig. 25)
Oil on canvas, 21⅜ x 17⅜ inches
Rijksmuseum, Amsterdam